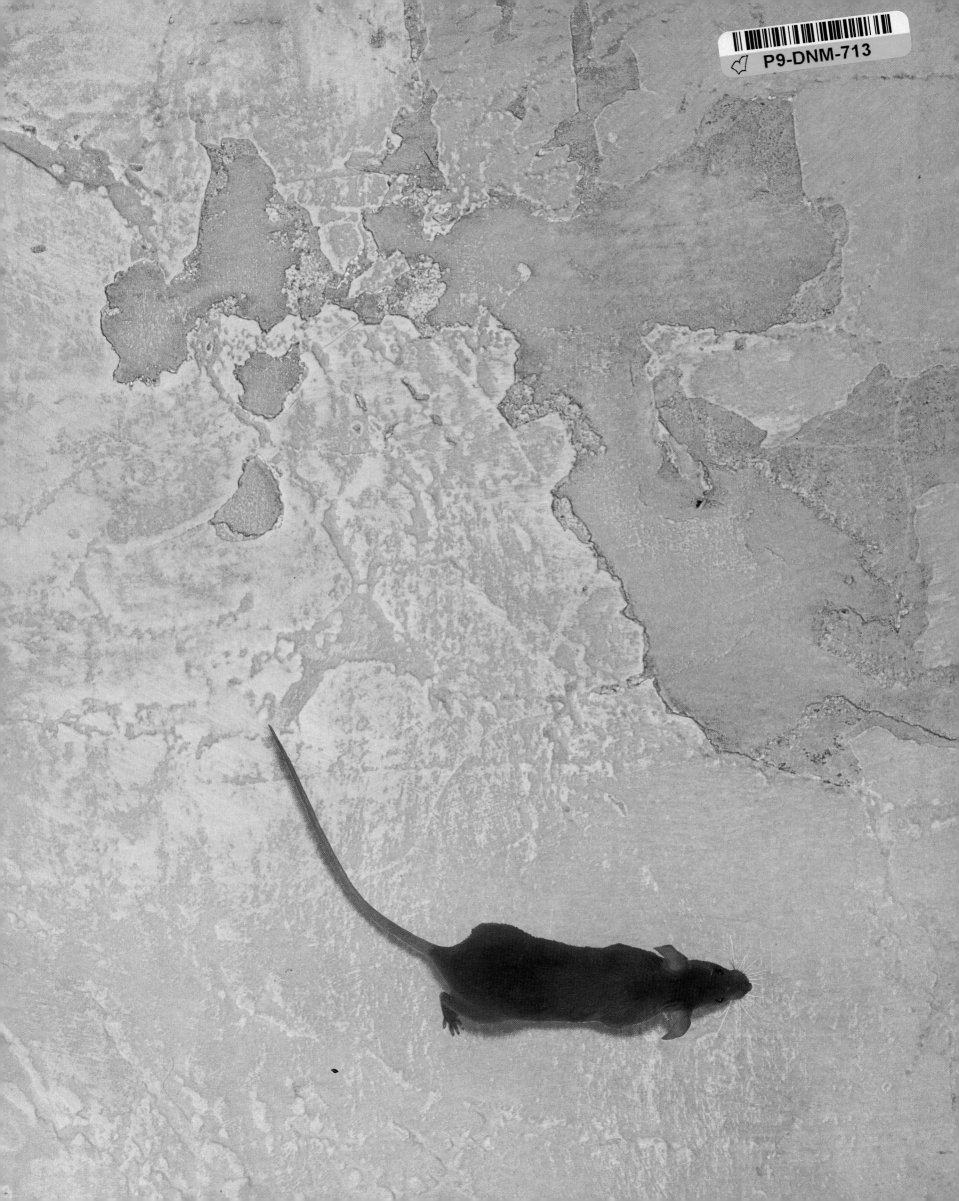

A DK PUBLISHING BOOK

Project editor Miriam Farbey
Art editor Karen Fielding
Designer Mary Sandberg
Stylist Marion McLornan
Photography Tim Ridley
Production Louise Barratt
Photographer's assistant Nick Goodall
Additional photography Dave King
US editor Camela Decaire
Consultant Dennis Severs

Dorling Kindersley would like to thank Borderline, A. D. Carpets, Clifton Little Venice, Faith Eaton, Carole Handslip, Simon Money, Neal's Yard Dairy, Pearl Cross Antiques Ltd., Robert Purves, V. V. Rouleaux, and Paul Scannell for their help in producing this book. Silver supplied by Langfords, in the London Silver Vaults. Meadow set designed and made by Rocky Road Productions Limited.

First American Edition, 1995
2 4 6 8 10 9 7 5 3

Published in the United States by
DK Publishing, Inc., 95 Madison Avenue
New York, New York 10016

Library of Congress Cataloging-in-Publication Data
Henrietta.
   A country mouse in the town house / by Henrietta. — 1st American ed.
      p.   cm.
   Summary: After a harrowing visit to the city, a peace-loving mouse
decides that she prefers her quiet life and simple food in the
country.
   ISBN 0-7894-0021-9
   [1. Mice—Fiction.   2. Stories in rhyme.]   I. Title.
PZ8.3.H419Co   1995
[E]—dc20
                                                                    94-37526
                                                                       CIP
                                                                        AC
Color reproduction by Classic Scan, Singapore
Printed and bound in Italy by L.E.G.O.

🐭 Follow the trail of five green peas in every picture.

🐭 Search carefully for the mice hidden in each scene.

A COUNTRY MOUSE IN THE TOWN HOUSE

by

Henrietta

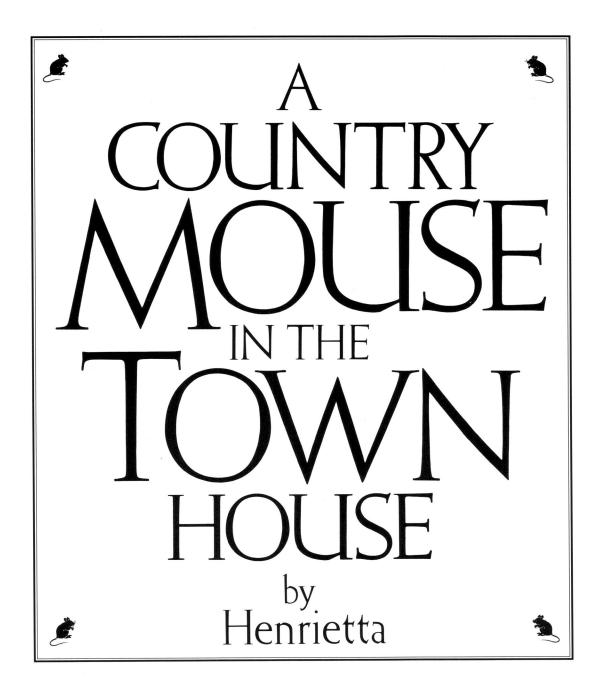

In a snug country cottage a fat little mouse
Enjoyed, undisturbed, the whole range of the house;
With plain food content, she would breakfast on cheese,
She dined upon berries, and supped on green peas.

$\mathscr{A}$ friend from the town to the cottage did write:
"Leave your forests and fields for the city's delights;
Why not come to the town, as quick as you please,
I'll treat you to more than mere berries and peas."

$\mathscr{T}$his kind invitation she could not refuse,

And the country mouse wished not a moment to lose;

She rushed to the kitchen, provisions to seize,

A snack for the journey—some berries and peas.

A cartload of produce was headed for town;
The little mouse crept in and settled right down,
And, saying good-bye to the fields and the trees,
She was glad that she had her ripe berries and peas.

$\mathcal{T}$o the town house she came, wriggled under the door.
"Come in!" cried the town mouse. "See what I've in store;
With me shall you feast just as long as you please,
Come, leave those old berries and horrid green peas.

"Here are custard and trifle, and cheesecakes galore,
Nice candies and cookies, and twenty things more,
Elegant dishes designed just to please,
Far better than berries and boring old peas."

They were merrily munching when into the room
Came the dog and the cat, and the maid with her broom.
The mice in a fright through a small hole did squeeze;
How the country mouse sighed for her berries and peas.

As they fled through the drawing room, she cried, "Away!
I can venture no longer in this town to stay,
For if oft you receive interruptions like these,
I would far rather have my plain berries and peas."

own House
London

I can hear something
scratching.
There must be mice
in the house!
I wonder where
they are hiding?

They hid in a room full of toys bright and gay,
But the cat with the mice was more eager to play;
With tightly shut eyes and trembling knees,
The country mouse yearned for sweet berries and peas.

They scrambled upstairs, scuttled onto a bed:
"Let's make our escape," the country mouse said.
"I want to go home to the flowers and trees,
And, best of all, to my berries and peas.

"Through fields and through meadows come let us scurry;
Run faster, dear friend, we really should hurry,
Or late we shall be for our breakfast of cheese,
And our dinner of berries, and supper of peas.

" *Y*our living is splendid and gay to be sure,
But the dread of disturbance you ever endure.
I taste true delight in contentment and ease,
And live happy forever on berries and peas."